AVERAGE HEIGHT OF FLIGHT

Caitlin Press Inc.
8100 Alderwood Road,
Halfmoon Bay, BC V0N 1Y1
www.caitlin-press.com

Text design by Benjamin Dunfield
Edited by Patricia Young
Cover design Vici Johnstone
Cover art by Chris Maynard
Printed in Canada

Caitlin Press Inc. acknowledges financial support from the Government
of Canada through the Canada Book Fund and the Canada Council for
the Arts, and from the Province of British Columbia through the British
Columbia Arts Council and the Book Publisher's Tax Credit.

Canada Council Conseil des arts
for the Arts du Canada

BRITISH COLUMBIA
ARTS COUNCIL
An agency of the Province of British Columbia

Library and Archives Canada Cataloguing in Publication
Kope, Beth, 1959-, author
    Average height of flight / Beth Kope.
Poems.

ISBN 978-1-927575-68-0 (pbk.)

    I. Title.
PS8621.O68A94 2015   C811'.6   C2014-907947-8

AVERAGE HEIGHT OF FLIGHT
Beth Kope

CAITLIN PRESS

Acknowledgements

To those who encourage and support me in the craft of writing:
Arleen, Isa, Sue, Betsy and my wise and skillful editor Patricia.
To those who support me in the craft of life:
Lia, Pat, Helene, Janet, Bernadette, Eileen,
Joan, Mary, Alice, Mairi, Nicole, Suzanne.
Thanks be.

To Harry, Meghan, Nina, Everett and Al with love. Family.
And for Shady, by my side.

CONTENTS

I
LAND (OF DOMESTICA)

GOD IS A RABBIT

Did you know that in our first weeks of life, we see upside down?
Then our brains learn to turn.

So there's a hole
and the hole isn't black

and the sky isn't blue. It is the water in the atmosphere
that refracts light and so we see

blue.
Blue.

My cousin was eight when she got her first pair of glasses:
all the way home, exclaimed at her new world.

Trees weren't giant mushroom blots but distinct ingredients
of jade, pine, teal and

her mother's fur coat wore gazillions
of jet-black shafts and

the familiar smudges of family translated
to moving mouths, eloquent eyebrows.

Her mother
wept at all that had gone unseen.

This is a true story.
Hope hops among us

and god is a rabbit. From a certain paw, light, tail, flush
burrowed and hidden

until we see
forest ways and meadow grass bendings.

FOLLOWING NOSE OF DOG PATH

1. THETIS LAKE LOOP

What did I think of?

One echoing house. Empty of my mother. Boxes to be filled.
One precarious child. Waiting to ambush me.
One bloody train wreck. This, my life.

I am back at the car   keys in hand   but how?

I haven't seen

lake

sky

trees

path

have not left one harrowed moment behind.

2. LONE TREE

From the familiar, my feet turn
onto a deer path, not knowing
how high it curves

pursuing the ridge.

The dog is happy. New route, new smells.

Never mind deer trails disappear —
this one concealed by fallen maple leaves
and expanses of moss-slick rock:

the path splits like snarled capillaries
forking
forking, which one to
the heart?

3. FROM MUNN'S TO MILLSTREAM

Spruce   apron moss   hemlock   maidenhair fern   cedar.

Dead standing trees.

Rotten logs   windfall   crisscross path.

Sea serpent roots cresting   fallen fir needles and mud.

Windlaunched jilted branches   loose stones.

Spruce   apron moss   hemlock   maidenhair fern   cedar.

Windfall crisscross my path.

4. Off Seaborn Trail

On the lip of a cliff, about to chase another route
down and realize
they would find my car, but not me, me in a heap
at the bottom.

What am I thinking? That my
aging knees can hurtle my body down rock face?

No trail behindinfronttotheside
I am lost
brought to this ledge.
Brought
to this edge holding grief, the effort of grinding legs and lungs.

5. Short Cut Off McKenzie Creek Trail

Full crash
into salal
up to my chin

can't find my feet

can't find the trail

deep in green

barely make sky

every step thornyknotted

6. MUIR CREEK TRAIL

A passage up cascades
falls   still pools

through the channel of hunkering forest
        in trembled green avenue.

The undulating trail lays bare
boulders surfacing for air
   the mud   the sand

and paths turn swelling creekbeds
from rain, leaving
         flat stones   round stones

precarious roots my feet slur past.

7. FRANCIS KING

leaf, leaves

leaves behind me

leaf   leaves

leaves me behind

8. CRAIGFLOWER CREEK TO PRIOR

slide
as foot hits
sly wet root

and skids.

9. TRILLIUM TRAILHEAD

I have looked up the name for this moss, each time
I forget. It is a small island, its own universe.

CARCASS ON THE BEACH

(that my dog rolled in)

Laid out
on sand, heron
wings arch lightly
in balletic brackets
feathers still tether wings
in an innuendo of flight.

Great horny toes
stretch en pointe.
Curved beak
too long to believe.

What caught her, lowered
her with ripping teeth, left her rib cage cleaned
by crow
suppliant, suppliant
        like fingers arched in prayer?

Friend's Funeral

What she could have said
at his funeral, spoke
aloud the moment
he touched her wrist
across the kitchen table.

That day's simple comfort.

The last time another human
touched her:
centuries ago.

To the House of Wooden Floors

She thinks of leaving her house with wood floors
and kind light keeping company all day

certainty of views from windows
closeness of the bathroom in the night.

yes   no   yes   now

This house has nineteen years of children's scuffle
and door frames notched with inches grown.
There is all she will miss
all she can do without.

Uncertainty moves in:
she's pinned to this small lot.

What happened to her nomadic garb
and frayed backpack?

FORECAST

Po pulls apart and the bed splits up to the skin.
— I Ching

If you wish to forecast the future
choose six yarrow sticks pared to white bone
or toss thumb-worn coins. With every throw
hold the question in your fist.
Keep still.

If you wish to forecast the future
try the smoky tea room, ask the Roma.
Her hands lay the cards, find what you fear
and pray for, a Tower falls and Lovers
pierced by three Swords.

The future, it's there, in your grip, turn it over.
Your left hand what you're born with
the right what you've done.
How to untangle those three fate lines
that chart your centre palm?

Look to stars. Pour tea.
Bring home beach stones, their stripes map what you need.
Ask geese. Count crows in the sky.
Bite cake, sleep with it under your pillow.
Open the Bible at random.

You look into the soap suds in the sink
think broken plate, bent fork.
Read between rumpled lines
of sheets on the bed
and realize you can step out the front door.

Dog Tribe

When I walk two dogs, I am in tribe, honorary four-legged.
Dogs and I outside notions of body, notions of two vs. four.
Halt for vigorous sniff at base of tree, under log;
brown pup shoots after smell trails.

Dogs and I, outside, as one
old girl wheezes at my heels
can't catch this bolt shot from cannon, so fast
back legs scramble to keep organized.

Old girl wheezing, walloped as pup passes.
The dogs and I out, lakeside.
 Wish I could jump in, no pelts of clothing to shed:
back legs scrabble to break, he is ahead behind ahead behind
just how in four-legged dreams I careen through brush: tear skin.

Dogs and I side by side: could I jump this bluff?
How at thirteen — really eighty — old dog clambers any rock face. I wish.
In dreams I bolt rip bomb through underbrush
dream a four-legged dream.

Thirteen is eighty, she scrambles hurtles full tilt til
adjourning for sniffs at trees and logs.
I dream four legs.
In the company of two dogs, I am in tribe.

STOPPED AT RUSH HOUR ON HELMKEN OVERPASS

A lofting of homing pigeons
         plumage starched
loosened
      from their dovecote
bound by infinitesmal weft
both in flight and aloft.

Give me the music
        composer scored
with these perched
notations
matched to each pigeon

chording in fifths on wingtip and
dominant sevenths of beak and

let it trill, vibrato against spines
          of feathers
belt it out while pigeons pause
        for hums beneath gnarly feet
gripping telephone wires
        dark strokes on blue sheet music.

Give up to diminuendos
        of orchestrated swoops.
Give in:
     let regret migrate south
          along those songs in minor keys

a practice session of scales in migration.

VANTAGE

Even the air has changed, sliding into fall
coolness as the sun moves further below the hill.

I reach the crest below power lines, catch
the wind circling the nape of the hill like a scarf.

The sky leans against horizon, blends
late purple light from texture to cobalt.

Somber shadows of red aspens and cedars
stretch across the cutline.

Grass stalks quiver.

There is one full minute of silence from the crows.

Deer Become True Only

In the hour of dusk entre chien et loup
I walked through forest back to the truck
eye-strain, foot-falter on craggy trail.
Two conspiring hints
deer line   deer contour
tread onto the path ahead
and dog   halts   sits   unheard of.

We are where old tales hold fast
riddles run through forest on spectral feet
these strange unloosened souls.

We are where deer become true   at the moment of their leap.

TRANSLATION RAVENSPEAK

Raven's voice disguised as a bitter startled bell
lured me with lament, script wound round me.
A blindfold, a ribbon circling a finger.

Raven's accusations are all the goodbye
notes ever, words written in black feather.

Who would translate? The scripture
within has fled. For surely
the ground has swallowed her whole.

WHEN SOLACE ADMITS NOTHING

I wash my sister's naked body..
Stroke is not a gentle word.
Soap on steamy washcloth, soap at the ready
I swab her back, rinse, my arm bracing
her leg, glissade of urgent balance.
I cup one foot, the other, offer
my shoulder, struggle to project solidity

though the weight of sustaining
is much more than she weighs.
We make a crowd, bump elbows
the shower stall so small water spills spray.
She leans   nearly loses   grips my forearm
turns her head with eyes blown helpless.

This was not supposed to happen.
There are no words to reassure, jokes to push past.
I'm implicated in exposure:
her nakedness unfamiliar.

Along our fencelines we have chosen silence:
of broken   of weakening.
Of scrunched pillows running the middle of the bed
the wall built to keep cold feet from drifting
to a sister's body heat in the night.

SEYMOUR HILL

1. AT THE TOP

Your small slit eye against the sky whispers
its secret surrendered.
                         Of geese
tripping over the lake below me
an unravelling line of feather that stitches
pull and wind direction. Hunger. Parasites.

            What is it to you, moon,
on top of Seymour Hill out of reach
                         of pine arms?

I have come
to lick this evening
dusk folding us crisp.
Shiver with geese

repeat feather and bone
treble and bass
hint and hit.

                 What is it to us, moon, feeding
on every living thing?

2. COMING DOWN

By the time I reach Seymour Hill
I am sole witness
as the weak-kneed sun
is palmed by the pines
in a magician's sleight of hand
          (to be swallowed
by his lovely assistant)

It's 4:14 p.m.
Tomorrow's light hours are one minute, five seconds less
and I blunder
downhill in this nether light.
Won't make it to the top of Seymour Hill until spring.

3. AT THE BASE

Rain falls
anchor to the seabed, burrows deep
entering silt and sand
skin and eyes
a relentless toss to saturated paths
land guzzling this pummelling rain.
The lake is higher than I've ever seen.

What change of fortune?
What change in weather?

A heart-shaped leaf
floats on the lake's surface
wind-coaxed to the shore
to my outstretched hand
pushes off from my fingertips:

DIALECT

Are you god or trickster? One of the damned, ghost of murdered
soul?   If I ate your heart

        you ate mine
what would be the last word on my tongue, from your wide beak?

You have a thousand words.
I can't interpret three.

Scolding know-it-all, taunter of eagles   hawks
rattling them with your keck-keck-keck alarm.

You proselytize on stone dropped
through deep water, chant;   er-WAH er-WAH   er-WAH

release your scale of glottal sobs
from your flight path to the ridge

vibrato leaving your throat, rasping the valley
a metallic clang of steel against teeth.

Hold on   hold on   hold on
oh AHHHHH   oh AHHHHH   oh AHHHHHHH

OF ONLY THIS NOVEMBER

Once the park was full of them: leafy trees
blankets, tussling children, tipped
lemonade cups and grape stems in small heaps:
an infrastructure of ease.

Today the wind chafes the ground
leaves sort themselves in gutters
the scraps and rags of a hero's coat
blown from broad oak backs.

Shelter. Shelter. Each mammal needs the hole, the roof.
The sanctuary of eaves.

II
LIFT

Quest

Go to the forest, where none may pass.
There is no trail to follow
nor any trail back. So make a pact or take a risk
on a fox, a bee, the chance your guide is disguised.
Your journey brings cold. Hunger rides piggyback.
Fires won't blaze in the rain.

Search until you find
a low river rebounding its banks
shadowed by tightly overgrown branches.
Step into the water. Kneel.
Grip the rocks in your hands

and lie face down. Become
part, the current
the path you stepped off
questing.

Trailing Enchantment

My father's days unfold though the curtains never open.
He sits undressed, bedside
frozen in that moment when his finger
pricked the spindle.
So tall, yet when he falls, bewitched
under the spell
he goes down like the beanstalk, like the giant
shredding earth.

He hides beneath the robe of enchantment
it is paisley, hanging to his knees.
We have no proof it is him at the dinner table, silent.

Morning glory tendrils push through the floor
an army of vines threading their way up table and chair legs
coiling vines inch up the stairs
to the bedroom where he lies or sits
eyes drawn in on the spell of stillness.

I pull the vines until my palms weep green
but every day I find new growth, fresh flowers
open-mouthed across his chest.

MINK VIGNETTES

In inquisition of mink, such is fearless.
Boldest. Will follow me down;
owns trail.

On encounter with ruthless black
(such is one slink mink)
never flung afar from
(this lake that seasonal stream)
discharged dart
over moss slopes and loose turned logs
over shoulder.
Watch me.

Once
diving frigid ocean after eel in sleek swim
stub-legged
part web-footed
easy effort from green algae-wrapped boulder crevice.

Once from packsacks to bags
midday midsummer amid teens at lake edge;
whose lake?!
So much for the wary: only hardnosed audacity
shameless theft on mind.

And off in deepest brush, my dog brashing about,
scent searching, suddenly crossing trail at my feet: a carousel.
In lead,
rabbit   from wet brush to deep scrub uphill
mink   from wet brush to deep scrub uphill
dog   from brush to scrub
dog   veers
                      tack   back
stalled at my feet, panting.

SUITE: DESPAIR

1. WHEN THE VOLCANO DUST SETTLES ON AN INDONESIAN ISLAND AND THE TV SHOWS WHITE GHOSTS

Regard less

As if eyes coaxed shut
black scarf taut.

As if dark
could not be lit again:

the sun
ten centimetres further

gone, too
candles and lamps

ears close over
brim with salt

sound suspends
mouths latch shut.

The list of what is missing amasses; light and
safe haven and

food, water.
Now, barely air, as

arms of black plumes
stretch skyward.

When home is not.

2. REWRITING

Let's start this poem with an eraser. It's a useful tool
will improve our lives, start
with the words in the newspaper article.
Let's erase
stepped off the bus. No
she didn't.
And so we can erase the other words that come after; like *held*
and *tied* and *knifed* and *burnt.* Where is it written
that this had to? This is where our eraser comes in handy
again and again. Erase *and then she was gone*
or *they never saw her again.*
It isn't foolish hope.
I have already begun on today's paper. Here
you do yesterday's.

3. CHEMO

Maybe galaxies die behind our eyes and cause our moments of abysmal,
complete despair. Then, though still ignorant, we would at least be grand.
—R.M. Kinder

Maybe, she says, she'll try rock climbing
to conquer her fear of dangling. Says she'll buy
expensive wines to drink on the spot, avoid aging vinegar surprises.
Maybe there will be alicewonderland sips, prescriptions that
stretch her (blood) vessels in compromise.
Maybe galaxies die behind her eyes.

Didn't the last MRI show black holes and constellations
ripening in her body? All her anatomy is in a state of repair
sharing solar systems of modus formulas.
She tries to muffle the hectic sounds of scaffolding
under construction inside her, unfamiliar
causing moments of complete despair.

Although she has hope, it's thin. Sometimes only a drop of salt water.
She's burnt by intravenous interventions, mired in demands her body begs
from her: shit and act of, hair loss means constant nose drips—just supplant
them all with radiant thoughts. Believe you're in control.
Sometimes no words can reach, sometimes A Good Long Rant.
Then, though still ignorant

laugh.
Hey, who knows, really: hairs on each head, hour of death, sparrows
that stand, fly or fall? Search internet or blogs, bibles
of any persuasion, find the command for fairy-tale endings
or just know. Whatever may be
she is grand.

HIDDEN

Furrowed field lines
of curved black waves
break and roll.

Let the earth breathe steam.

A red fan-tailed hawk
sweeps by tree-tip to fence.

Small things below may pause
but what is hidden
will work to the surface.
Reach down
take hold of the trembling moment
white, on your palm.

FALLEN

Snow has drifted shut the front door.
I let the dog out the back way.

Our yard has become strange
territory.

This landscape is a tightly stretched sheet
stolen from our bed.

IN SCALE OF WHITE

—in the nineteenth century, Wilson Bentley photographed and published
thousands of images of snowflakes, died in a snowstorm

His days defined
by beauty that disappears
at touch of earth, of eyelash, captured
crystals before warmth won.
He could list families of design, lineage of line, snare
one crystal. One more. Another
all frozen on black photographic plates
to seize their hearts.
One more. Another. He begged
the sky, send more
one thousand, four thousand

each flake tumbling, hurtling to tongue and face.
Shape.
Let.

This is the scale white music plays.

What My Teenager Tells Me

You tell me, your words
flung cross the kitchen table
but I can't read
don't know how
to interpret fists
spelling, letters tossed
past your shoulder
that orbit your body
speed too quickly.

You tell me in notes
disguised as folded bookmarks
left for me to open, flatten
and with the wet of my tongue
try to dissolve the ink
until I taste blue and
leave the paper clean, pristine
the way I
hope to find you.

You tell me to translate the lines
on your shins
eloquent as red
ink brush strokes
on rice paper.
Tell me
this is hardly the world
for a child
with porous skin.

TO HOLD THOSE GONE

This raven's passing wing brushes my shoulder
loops back to light on a branch
the way my father's final exhalation of blood
was taken by wind breath.

To hold those gone, some press flowers, frame photographs.
I scrawl his name on an envelope, send
directions for the route back, maplines
seen from raven's vantage point, a topography of love.

Tell me.   What are poetic truths?
How far to Winnipeg? Why does blood stain?
And where do frogs go, or souls, to hibernate in winter?

THE EVENING VISITOR

At the moment the sun crash-lands against the horizon
the sky turns lilac, blue-lipped and hums.

Eyes, stunned by this sudden dimming light
seek to make sense of it all.

The rock, a bear waiting to crash from brush.
The dog at the far end of the ice-bound lake is a startled wolf.

The priest is an illness
kneeling bedside.

Doubting our eyes' message
we can only guess.

The evening visitor approaches the door.
Before he knocks and comes in from the cold

before the candle is lit, the lamp switched on
when the answers in books are out of reach

tell me

who is this with bread and wine
coming with mud over his eyes?

Who comes with death on his arm?

BARGAIN

Dog paws compress
my chest. I inhale sadness
from its wretched breath, wake with black dog saliva
trailing cross my pillow.

Dog hunts fragility
avid to lunge down my throat
chase to ground, chew to bits.
I am shredded.
A hound herds my thoughts, my sheep knees
tremble.

These days two black dogs shadow
my path. I gamble reckless
rabbit scents or the kill a turkey vulture circles
will lure this terror
and I tear back tothetrailtothecarlockdoor
bargaining the beast won't track
my spoor, circle back to lie, implacable
on my front step.

MEDITATIONS ON DISTANCE

Imagine the fetch, where waves have finally found safe harbour:
and the farthest pocket palm of land is surrounded by countless days.

Your fork.
My spoon.

At a party, the air crazed with music and chat.
No one leans in close.

Of the first step, of the slide to the bottom. Of the dream of a fall.
Of the land(ing). Hard. Oh.

Try to make sense of the child that spurns.
Cross this trepidatious ocean.

Wind carries birds blown by happy accident to their new isle.
Seeds are summoned or hidden in feathered bodies.

Such are the navigators who trust stars
squint into sun.

The dead wait on distant shores
claim the right gift.

Tracing a petroglyph, the chiselled mystery of a monstrous squid
with a human face.

As the crow flies.
To the moon.

Measured with tape or bearing compass
of landmarks or celestial bodies.

From confines of cave depths, from hairpin turns up the steepest scarp
the heart flounders.

      Horizon: it is only apparent
supposed.

It's offing of sea to sky (from the summit of Seymour Hill)
many many more miles from here.

To My Aging Dog

The last time you retrieved sticks from the lake, over a year
      no more bobbing black head legs paddling full on.
Last time you swam? When I went out and you rescued me
      refusing to stay on shore.
Last time you jumped out of the car
      hips crumpled.
Last time you jumped in the car
      you hung, obliged to accept a boost.
The last time we saw a rabbit, you bounded two leaps forward, but
      no disappearing act or ardent yips from brush.
The first time you peed in the house
      recurs. Recurs.
Hearing going, eyes clouding, muzzle and ears and belly graying
      and those farts.
You haven't heard old dogs lose appetite, read the clock, riled if we're
      slow.
Wake at 4:45 a.m. to check the yard out, sit on the back stoop, watch for rats.
      And pee.
Wake at 5:14 a.m.
      And pee.
Last time you chewed a bone, months ago: teeth ache
      worn down.
Wheeze all walk long right at my heels or lag, sniff lost in smell, then
      where is that darn human?

Last time I came in the house you lay on the couch (never would before)
      tongue lolling.
I stroked you,
      hoped you were only sleeping.

III
A (Loft)

WHAT COULD BE MORE ALLURING THAN THE TIDES?

we have tabled them and measured neap with moon
cycled and counted. but sit
beside the sea, tell me your eyes
aren't shocked as it slides away so steadily?
just minutes ago that boulder was hidden.
coast grows, sand spreads, rock revealed.
the distance to the waterline retreats, retreats.
slick algae sheen, stranded starfish and kelp beds
scent the air as the sun warms them.
what was the break of a whale's back cresting offshore
is now an island. this is a game of red light
try to catch the moment ocean slackens.
suddenly there is silence.
the shore bends, tide holds before it turns, and then
turns. gulls collide with barnacle-crusted rock and sob.
wing tips slap water. when i look again
the sun has pushed the ocean nearer.

THANKS BE

For the years I followed your nose
followed your paws
shadowing your waveflagtail
through storms of flung branches
gyrating treetops, rain biting deep
through languid spokes of days.
Geography and the spell
of seasons unfurled before us.

You immersed me in doctrine of deep forest
ravines, unmapped creeks.
We built psalms from seasons.
Sight was all to me:
you built chapels of scent.
I tracked your trails, bent to your ways.
I was the apostle with belief
in joy of lost.

Thanks be to dog.

Score of the Land

Remember once there was no
border   nor fence   nor have:
        forest
was forest.
My feet paid tribute
traipsing over red-button snails
translucent pistachio-green sluglettes
honouring hill top moss that two steps crush forever.
Ignoring swooping c swirls of barbed wire
rusted to stump-rot poles, loose flagging tape.
Markers, unremarkable, unmarking
I knew deer stepped lightly over.
An unnamed creek ran the ravine untouched:
has it only been one year?

Witness the land scored
with knives riding in on wheels two storeys high
trees altered to heaps one storey high, wrenched
discards. On burning nights, I stood
at the fenceline on my watchtower
kept vigil as they turned spirit, left this earth behind.
Changes charge at, regroup; fences up. Trees down.
A high ridge once hidden by a family of bearded cedars, bereaved
after their plunge down the cliff, ripping a laneway for other
wreckage, the creek smeared
(tires, wrapped and rusting metals, all in a strange language of disuse)

On the path one day I found the dead fawn
 tossed from their side to mine
and through the months, a blasting reshuffling of earth
what was pond is twice as large
edged in boulders.
Once hill shredded to the ultra-green-grassed 17th hole.
What is the score?

NESTING

Morning, with snow still
lying flat in the yard's shadows, the mother
sends the girls out, tasked
to find anything they would use
if they were birds building nests. Such
serious searching. She watches, coffee
mug in hand, her forehead
pressed to cold glass.

They forage in bushes, collect the expected—
twigs, long grass stalks and who
will carry clay from the rock garden—
the smallest now cups a frozen clump
—grass-leaves-twigs-pine needles-an old feather-dog's hair
(black nap, wiry and undercoat fluff)—more twigs—
and when they come in, the girls are red raw
and hunt for pictures of finch abodes, of robin saucers—
        the startle of elaborate grass socks swinging
of constructed pendants and knitted spheres
        (not the nests of scrape or mound
or platform, cavity or cup)

They are keen to try next steps:
        find a forked branch
        use all nesting materials
        weave
        as if with a beak:
using hands not as adept as beaks

it is a joke. Stack and shaping
pile a home for —
imagine — ovoid and elliptic
could be speckled, could be blue
home for the broken robin eggshell
found on the front step
and the blown green eggs
from the neighbour's pullet.

NESTS

The mother hears a webcam
is aimed at an eagle's nest.
People with time on their hands
watch throughout the nights, the days
the feeding, the foraging, the cleaning and guarding;
until the nest gives way. A storm
shook loose the layers and layers of collected branches, or
a tree rot finally won or
there is no shelter.

   The mother tells her daughters to fill their nests
with bright jelly beans and foil-wrapped eggs.
Tells herself
their own nest will not collapse.

FAMILY DINNER

Last night we ate at the kitchen table, a bit
of a squeeze, our hands could all touch in the middle, if we'd wanted.
The curry nourishing and we talked
of recent visits to dying family:
aunt, sister, stepdad, of bad choices and coming losses, drinking
and estranged sons in Miami. Of cancer and statistics.

There was a baby coming, my hand landed on flutters
belly ripplings, crazy bumpings.
She said there are times it's a wave beneath skin.
I said no, a marine mammal carried by the wave, the otter
waiting to come to land.

Crows began staging in the Garry oaks
out back. They unsettled, then settled, unravelled and launched.
Someone mentioned the night last summer
when for two hours crow clouds flew in, endless family
clans churning the dusk until the cobalt wash hinted at dark
and they found their way home.

EVERYTHING COSTS

She said here's the thing about laundromats;
they're a great place to meet lonely men except
you only go when your washing machine dies, so
there is the sadness of broken.

Or you never had a washing machine, so there is
the sadness of no money, and everything costs, like those tiny
boxes of Cheer.
But the hot air, regardless, the steaming windows —
it's an expedition in a soiled jungle.

She said her heart is coin-operated, said
she sorts darks and whites, separates
colours but there's never enough
for one fair load and they go in with the whites too
so why bother sorting, go ahead, try to
find a free machine
and never leave someone's
wet clothes on a dryer, as she
folds the make-do bit by bits
smoothes out her losses.

BIRD IN BUSH: THOU SAYEST

I don't know brush signals or alarms but you are there, tucked in deep.
Thou sayest thy piece, camouflaged, but
if I am being warned not to come nearer, I am clueless.
If it's a complicated love song playing in the key of steamy viridian green
I wouldn't know

but if you wrote it in Braille, my palm would brush feather
smooth ruffled nervousness
light on rapid-beat roundness, my fingertips linger

over eye bead
          reading
                    meadow grass tips sifted with delicate midges

over head crest
          reading
                    a summons for love weaving branchlets to homenestness

over tail plume and tip
          reading
                    liftoff shaft arrow shaft rachis quill mark.

Thou sayest all this in thy body: thou sayest
hawk circle cower
fevered nest building
bliss for spring sun breaking through rain clouds
guard of the legged coming closer to salal.

Thou sayest.

ZEN OF DROPS

1.
Rain droplets shiver on my kitchen window.
Suspense.
Once one releases
others follow.

2.
I live in a rainy city
yet I walk out the door
with no umbrella.

3.
Asleep in the attic.
Rain lulling
sleepers with footfalls.

4.
Rain splatter clouds blow in
blow out
shut down the days. I swim
through damp air.

5.
Lichen. Old man's beard.
Both abundant.
Look, all the moss caps
blown from my roof.

6.
A land saturated
a land awash,
my chest,
heavy until tears come.

PREDICTION

This tree sprang from bird shit
burrowed in and found good ground
grew like a weed.
By the time we noticed
too big for replanting.
It fills the yard with roseblush white, volume
set on high vibrato, bees and flies and all
manner of humbuzzing.

Our legless neighbour predicted the first windstorm
would lay it flat, yet it stands
unidentified; laden with oblong burgundy fruit.
It will not give way.

SAANICH BUCKS ENTANGLED

When you stepped into view through the boiling mist in the low field
my heart lurched for a joust. Over sex, territory.
You felt it too. That unreachable itch eased only by rough-barked fir
or tossing antlers. We measured the breaching distance
to each other's forehead: closing:
clash: retreat and clash and
with a throttled twist, combination lock, the tumblers closed.
Your neck twisted, my lean and shoulder-weight meshed:
we were bound, eye to eye in perplexed pause.

When you pulled back on your haunches I staggered
barely held, might have brought us both down.
We might have wrestled, kicking our pelts to shreds until the end
but somehow we held fast.
And now
this strange choreography
patterns our steps. We traverse fields   find water   sleep
upright and close
hope to break free of this bone-lock.

FOOLS FOR SPRING

(To be read at allegro presto presto, 280 words per minute)

Take the ram, or the ballerina dressed as ram
with the awkward thigh lump, curved hoof shoes
and one horn that unscrews to double as a phallus, well
some message is flooding
along with the Red River
against Fargo's sandbag banks, nothing wise or deliberated:
the ram is spring rite, right? hoofing it along with the twitter-twitt-
pate-ing of eagles, everywhere lust is spelled out.

A bit of warmth and earth reeks the air with lechery,
sweaters off, nylons, and who's wearing sandals,
glances on bared flesh,
there's no going back because Montreal's
unstacking chairs for outdoor patios. Baby lambs, baby lambs
humping. We stop every year to take pictures
but never mind, blurts the thrush through twigs in her beak
while mallards clobber each other
in ownership rites, and who thought to count blossoms
in the capital, wasted on lusty ballerinas
with bare chests, vigorous leaps cross the stage
staging virtuoso expression of Seed's raucous impulse; all
looking for a hefty, yes, strapping Nijinsky
to catch, kindle and hold.

SOLSTICE OWLS

In the kindled twilight of summer's eve, the sun is still hard at work.
You and I have left everything back at the trailhead.
Even our children. At the beach, they jump a solstice bonfire with friends.
Entering the forest, we see an owl take flight
its swoop of certainty.
Another follows through cedar.
We find them perched closer to the path than we dared hope.
One just above us, white rump rustling as it settles.

The sun has tarried all day.
It has unfettered the owls for they are effusive, fluent;
deep in their dialogue
of long days stretching into the hunt
grown owlets, another family out the nest
branches that sway with body weight.

We try to identify them from their feather-mapped markings,
tufts, vertical lines, golden eyes, shake out details that don't fit
but isn't it enough
that we heard their voices from beneath broadleaf maples?

ICON

I want to find a raven's skull cleaned of flesh
to hang above the kitchen door
to fill my hearth with ravenspeak.
Where do birds die?
Does raven hurtle to the ground
heart bursting, one wingbeat too many?
Or tip back off a branch
carving the air in a curling loop?
Should I hunt near cutlines
search tangles of fallen branches
or look on wind-notched hills
for raven's outline blanketed by beaked moss?
Will I find her on a storm-tinted beach
in tide's drifting brood, bleached clues
to tensile wingspan and chest breathe?

I leave the forest, drive home.
At the front gate, in my husband's palm, a songbird's skull.

GOOD DOG PATH

Jarring joints creak   stiff kneed   graying
muzzle   belly   tipped ears:
This mutt is aging.

She still bolts for the car but
won't lake swim in December
wheezes at my heels.

Old girl rarely chases scent or bush bashes.
Sees a deer, tips her ears, says
Oh.   Look.   Deer.

Wasn't that long ago she'd disappear
keep me posted on her progress
with joy-yips chasing rabbit.

What gifts she's given:
this good dog path, from home
to solitary stretches, past comfort

to trails of clamber and sweat, ambushed
by each season's flaunting:
calypso orchids   coral fungus bright orange

She's given need for new trails, for
owlsplurge   minktrip   cougarline   ravenspeak
For all that remains.

IV
A (Light)

Road Trip

1. Wire Pass, Arizona

Nothing is certain, nothing familiar.
At noon, the sky stretches white and sheer
fabric rippling overhead. The red
the red of slick rock scored by what unfaithful
water bullets through, unconstant.
Scored striated sandstone against your eyes
gorge walls braiding purple, orange, rust
and red hastening sun spears all below.
Deep in, the sky's iris above
you stop, drink again, water on neck, face
the trickle evaporates instantly.
You've been summoned to land where you know
nothing, play at pretence your feet belong.

Where the slot canyon widens to an alcove
scoured with bands of black: the sky returns.
You lean against rock, talus at your feet
and your finger finds one tiny perfect dot, another, follows
this ancient marked trail, the curve
leading you further, across desolation
and stone face to   petroglyph   desert bighorn sheep.
Others on the rock wall horizon
a herd yearning for motion.
Remember the shredding heat.
Light unyielding. Rock that bleeds red.
You left home for this arid place
that begs you eat stone, swallow dust.

2. A FURTHER

Another small town
coming up:
another three line poem.

> Speak to me.
> The way tires brush the road's surface.
> Constant.

I eat miles.
I am in Montana
after all.

> Perpetual wind
unabating (it preys on me
my altered state). I see

a mare locked against the wind
standing her ground in the untidy field, her back
opposing wind

tumbleweeds scoot across ahead. Prairie dogs
play chicken.
And there's   a gray barn

widening valley
narrowing valley
                          a gray house, lilacs in bloom.

> Another truck passes
The CD plays a story set in Brooklyn.

> How everything blurs.

                    The story, rain beading
the windshield, painted yellow lines, gas gauge, wind direction, creased
map unfolding secondary highways:

                              this is the road of my dreams and
I am waiting for a smaller breeze or silence or the next
. stop along the way.

3. DRIVING THROUGH

There is no place the wind does not scratch.
Cedargray posts slant, embraced by wind
in a backwards, choreographed dip.
Unrelenting blows, scraping surfaces
    combing grass
        tossing dust and earth skyward
into a scratchedwool scarf that wraps fields and slides
beneath doors, abrades exposed skin.
There is no place the wind does not scratch
grate the ground, shred the air.
What stands —structure or twisted flora or beast—
is whipped
fatigued by the chase.
Wind is a landscape,
land of its own scraping.
Wind is the moon eclipsing
the hills and the hand and the cattle and the
mare locked against it.
Wind is whistling chords
a haunt
so that what stands
is trapped in its excavations.

BONFIRE

with appreciation to Michael Crummey for his poem "Driftwood"

She tells me there are two seasons for bonfires:
the early spring
after winter storms have brought down
dead limbs, weak branches, toppled a whole tree
and late fall
garden bones of brambles, pruned branches
rotting wood from fences, steps, chicken coops.

She spends months in her many routes over the farm
dragging, wheeling, piling wood into a pyramid.
She loves hurling pieces higher, knows
it will be a three-day fire.
Early morning, she
crosses the wet grass in pink slippers
matchbox bumping in her sweater pocket.

She circles the cache, template of daily chores
finds the fragile space, pours gasoline
watches for the fire's conviction
and galloping pace. All afternoon, fire
throws sparks, twists in the back field.
She is welded to heat, knows all can be reduced:
consumed. Rise from ash.

FLASHLIGHT COLLECTION

Surely she will never give flashlights
at a funeral again, as if party favours
all of them retrieved from boxes of his collectables:
some retro black and chrome, some whimsies, the Aladdin's lamp
the death's head flashlight with laser filaments.

On the fridge, his old high school photo. He's bearded, high.
Old friends   come   go   stories spill
family   come   go   take   (only handfuls of)
still so much of him left; tools   boxes
the gate he hung last week
jars and jars holding aging flowers
white petals play mosaic on the table.

He swam too far.

Clematis petals like bruises surrender at the doorstep
blown into corners each time the door gusts
and a lickerish moth, thirsting for flame, brushes in.

Last night she attracted moths to her vine-draped
porch with the chrome Eveready beam
striating treetops, skimming grass.

He swam too far.

            What else for her to do but play flashlight tag
through rhododendron bushes,
calling all those children his, hers, borrowed, unborn.

FOREIGN TRAVEL

What a foreign way
to travel:

dipping   dip
submerged plunge   dunk
scull   lift in

canoe's transient tracks.

There's breath and wind:
muscle muttering   portages.

Such whimsy to these lakes
laid end to bend to
end

a watery silver frame around the bases of Tediko Peak
sentinel standing, needlepoint ridge.
This sliverous lake circuitry:

of Skoi and Babcock
spectacle of Lanezi and Isaac
tiny Kibbee.

Knee end to knee
chockablock with gear and all lashed in neat.

Tree speech translatable, just:
   during dark nights when the looming world leans
over to swathe us

and in the day, ice-age antlers beckon from lake deep, gestures
spanning eons
                       drop-offs into lulling stillness.

TENT SLEEP

This sleep
          is loon
how they send rippling 2 a.m. lake calls
          is owl
hunting and roused to smug
bone-crunching hoots
          is the drowsy air current alone along
hands, cheeks, beading condensation.

Over green ripstop nylon,
firs tip as if tent poles
a slight scythe of stars caught in the V.
Clean clouds fold
under the moon's sickle.
The wallowed weight of dark
presses a palm on this tent
empty of all scents but the forest out there
of all spun sound but
scurriness against a millimetre thick

—*could be*—
          —*could be*—

          needles set loose from a puny breeze
          clip of a cone against the ground
          cougar   bear   vole

This sliver of a shelter

          —*could be*—

a flimsy cobweb
porous as dreams in landscape
where meaning creeps
and scuttles out of sight

CROSSING THE CUTLINE

1.

I come with steady-paced feet and listen to my lungs' work
on this climb into exposed hilltops and wide views.

Chocolate lilies have spread
beyond the clutch I noticed long ago.
They've flourished in this clearing, a catchment for sun.

Late August and moss is scorched and brittle.
Every plant gulps moisture.
I rub my hands over the ground, absorb its fragile scent.

I came to walk hard, breathe hard
but the wounded can never escape their scars.

2.

I walk through one thousand tones and shades of green
the air visible to touch
the way two wingbeats of a swallow spell
hold on
release.
The zing of insects, electric bolts charge my skin.
Large purple dragonflies sail over the valley's salal.
The sun gathers strength, ironing flat our collective hurts.

3.

The cutline runs like an exposed spine, flanked by forest
down to the hollow small of its back
to the hill's shoulder blades
where cedars grow from its wing bones
green feathers rising
to catch the wind's orbits.

The cutline is interval and pause.
Sixteen ravens erupt.
The woodpecker's thrumming hits the metal struts of the hydro tower.
Insects crash past leaves, low flying, slightly dishevelled.

WHAT THE GEESE KNEW

I have left the creek below, through fir
to mossy crag. Cusp of summer
creek runs slower, but in this ravine
the air is porous.
Bursting through stillness, geese distress
flares from the flock down by the creek.
Such frantic clamour propels me downhill.

One goose, separated, blurts fearful pleas.
I hear her dragged from the creek through thick bush
up the ravine toward me.
These strands of prayer:
my running feet
the flock in outrage.

The flock lifts off in a black loop
a choir of lamentation.
Bereft. I don't see the cougar
that wrests her final breath:

the world skids, exhales silence.
Nothing to be done.

AVERAGE HEIGHT OF FLIGHT

The average height of flight of a robin is eight inches.
Robin, you disappoint.

Close to red fan-tailed hawk size
you claim only eight inches —
I can jump
higher.

Are you not trying
fraud of bird?

A waste
of wings, some say.
What are the other birds' averages?

Or perhaps statisticians haven't been
to my neighbourhood;

seen you topping the birch
bird determined upwards.

Here are your listings:

what wings resolve;

a perfect trajectory through brush
wingoars paddle air/body
distance + horizon = elevation
tree tip bending, wind
clambering

not thinking ground.

ONE STONE

One beach stone from among them all
will be the one your hand
reaches for
could fit beneath your tongue
surprise your mouth
could centre you.

Keep it in your pocket.
A bit of ballast.
Smoother than
greener than
blacker than

BLACKBERRY/STAIN

Sun-heavy blackberries tempt us to make a meal
of black juice and this sweet swaying perfume.
I could follow the thin fjords into brambles
from one berry to the next. But when to stop?

Take this one, it's ready to burst.
I'll dress your lips with it, like so, be
the wasp searching at the corner
of your mouth for summer.

DOGDOM

1.

Last night I dreamt
in four-legged scrabble, ran
with you, girl, the way you have
always, your nimble wit-darting
through bushes, up ridges. Such chase;
after rabbit, we did mink.
We ripped with teeth, tore
skin, reckless through brambles.

I was feral fur, wore
breath and bursts of speed.

2.

Sally Mann hung her dead greyhound in her barn
until skin dried, canine hair decomposed
beneath the hanging carcass. Bones
stacked, laid like yarrow sticks
to divine the future, focused in her lens.

And I say, tonight we run.
Tomorrow, I take your gray-powdered remains
run the ridge above the lake
then to three creeks.
I will run against wind to your favourites.

3.
At 3 a.m., my waking self
was halfway to the back door
summoned and certain
I'd heard you
(mysterious how such a gentle paw tap roused me night after night)
yet before I could stop, or say
isn't, I opened the door:
you wanted out.

Night air leapt at my knees, nipped my ankles and
you left, invisible as always against the back fence.

4.

Heartache is dogged.
Last night, I opened
the back door, begged for haunting.
Not a shadow.

Loss is never new.
Watch it sprint
like wind across grass in the field
turn solid ground to wavering ocean.

5.

(Call me Dogaressa)

Peggy Guggenheim's fourteen Lhasa Apsos
are buried next to her in a corner of her Venetian
garden. Better than any of Pollock's dribbles
they pulled her to the underworld
in a gondola, those darlings.

For anyone's palazzo full of art
is only home, only lively, because of
dog dog dog dog dog
dog dog. Times twice.

How I want you at my feet
waiting for me when I die.

ABOUT THE AUTHOR

Beth Kope has lived in Alberta, Quebec City and Australia and finds herself home in Victoria, BC, with her two grown, independent daughters, a grandson, lovely dogs and her husband. She supports students at Camosun College in Victoria.

Her first poetry book, *Falling Season* (Leaf Press, 2010), was built on the narrative of her mother's Lewy body dementia.

About the Cover Artist

Chris Maynard combines scientific knowledge, artistic sense, and a love of feathers and life in a new art form. His new book, *Feathers Form and Function* is a feast of art and writing about what feathers are, what they do, and why we find them alluring.

Artist Statement about Cover Image

I show feathers in new ways, cutting and arranging them in their three-dimensional forms. Each feather, though dead and discarded, keeps something of the bird's essence. Since I work mostly with shed feathers, some of the birds that grew them are likely still living.

This book is set in Arno Pro, designed by Robert Slimbach.
The text was typeset by Vici Johnstone & Benjamin Dunfield.
Caitlin Press, Spring 2015.
❧